Animals of the Night

BADGERS
AFTER DARK

Heather M. Moore Niver

Enslow Publishing
101 W. 23rd Street
Suite 240
New York, NY 10011
USA

enslow.com

Words to Know

gland—An organ in an animal's body that makes and gets rid of a product.

grasslands—Large open areas of land that are covered with grass.

habitat— The place in which an animal lives.

hibernate—To spend the winter sleeping or resting.

mammals—Animals that have a backbone and hair, usually give birth to live babies, and produce milk to feed their young.

nocturnal—Mostly active at night.

omnivores—Animals that eat both plants and animals.

predators—Animals that kill and eat other animals to stay alive.

prey—An animal hunted by another animal for food.

Contents

Badger Basics

Badgers are **mammals** and belong to the weasel family. They are related to ermines, mink, ferrets, martens, wolverines, and otters. There are eight species, or kinds, of badgers. They live in different **habitats**. They are various sizes and colors.

Badgers are strong. They have short necks and flat bodies. Badgers are great diggers. They have strong legs and long sharp claws.

Look underground to find a badger. They spend most of their lives down there. All badgers are **nocturnal**. This means they are most active at night. Badgers have scent **glands** near their rear ends. When threatened, they let off a stink!

FUN FACT!

Wisconsin's state animal is the badger. Miners once dug holes and tunnels. The tunnels reminded them of this underground creature.

Badgers are known for being rough and even nasty. This American badger got angry when it was disturbed while it was digging its burrow.

Meet the Badgers

American badgers live in North America. They make their homes in wide open areas of the country. Fields and meadows are some favorite spots. Their fur is gray or a mix of black and white. Their faces and feet are dark. A white stripe runs from its nose down its back. They eat mice, voles, gophers, and squirrels.

Eurasian badgers live in Europe and Asia. They sometimes live in the middle of cities. They have gray faces with black and white stripes. Eurasian badgers are **omnivores**. They like to eat rodents and small mammals. They also like to munch on fruit and nuts.

FUN FACT!

American badgers are usually about 23 inches (58 centimeters long). Their tail adds another 4 to 6 inches (10 to 16 cm). Eurasian badgers are 22 to 32 inches (56 to 81 cm) long. Their tails might be 5 to 8 inches (12 to 20 cm).

An American badger in Yellowstone National Park found a ground squirrel for its dinner.

Hog badgers are also called sand or hog-nosed badgers. Their behaviors are much like Eurasian badgers. But hog-nosed badgers have a piglike nose. They also have a long tail.

Hog badgers can be gray or black. Their heads are striped with black and white fur. Their throat, ears, and tail are white. Hog badgers are usually about 21 to almost 28 inches (55 to 70 cm) long. Their tail adds another 5 to 8 inches (12 to 20 cm).

These badgers usually eat animals like earthworms, but they also chow down on fruit and other small mammals.

FUN FACT!

A badger loves to eat earthworms! Many badgers will eat as many as several hundred earthworms in just one night.

Hog badgers make their homes in the mountains of southern Asia.

There are four species of ferret badgers. Some are called tree badgers or pahmi. The four kinds are Chinese, Burmese, Everett's, and Javan. They live in the **grasslands** and forests of India, Asia, and China.

Ferret badgers are smaller than American and Eurasian badgers. They are about 13 to 17 inches (33 to 43 cm) long, plus have a tail that is about 5 to 9 inches (12 to 23 cm). Most have brown to very dark gray fur.

At dinnertime, ferret badgers are omnivores. They like to eat insects, worms, small birds, rodents, and fruit.

Ferret badgers are among the smaller members of the badger family.

What's That Stink?

Malayan stink badgers live in the mountains on the islands of Asia. They are also called skunk badgers or teledus. Palawan stink badgers live in the Philippines. They are sometimes called Calamanian stink badgers. Stink badgers are usually between 15 and 20 inches (38 and 51 cm) long. They have a short tail. They weigh around 2 to almost 9 pounds (1 to 4 kilograms).

Stink badgers used to be considered part of the badger family. Recently, scientists decided stink badgers should be part of the skunk family. Their skulls and brains are like those of the stinky skunks.

Stink badgers are related to skunks. They both give off a mighty stinky stench!

Honey Badger's Got Time for . . . Honey!

The honey badger looks similar to American and Eurasian badgers. But honey badgers are more closely related to wolverines and martens. They are also known as ratels.

Honey badgers are usually between 24 and 30 inches (60 and 77 cm) long. Their tails add almost 8 to 21 inches (20 to 30 cm). Honey badgers usually live in Africa and southern Asia. Guess what they like to eat? You guessed it: honey! They also like to chow down on small mammals and fruit.

FUN FACT!

Some honey badgers are completely black. Most have a light gray or white head, neck, and back. Scientists think this coloring makes **predators** think it might not be a sweet snack.

A honey badger, or ratel, will eat almost anything. To find honey, it knows to follow the honeyguide bird. This bird will lead it to beehives.

Tough Guys (and Girls)

Badgers are rough and tough animals. They are able to fight off larger predators. Badgers will stand their ground against wolves, coyotes, and bears. Some badgers have fierce teeth.

Badgers are compared to bears sometimes. They are strong and muscular. Most badgers have short legs. But they are very strong front legs. Their front feet have long claws. (These are great tools for digging.) Badgers walk on the soles of their feet, just like bears.

Badgers are brave and strong. They will fight off bigger animals.

Secret Weapon

Badgers are tough, but they have another way to defend themselves. With a horrible stink! When they are scared or very excited, badgers can let out a liquid from glands by their tails. This is a lot like how skunks act when they are threatened or frightened. The smell makes the attacker back off. The badger doesn't seem like a tasty meal anymore! Badgers also use their scent to mark areas where they live.

When attacked, a badger might hiss, growl, squeal, and snarl. It will bite and use its long claws.

Home Sweet Home

Badgers live in the woods. They use their claws and strong arms to dig their homes, known as sets. Sets are also called holes or burrows. The burrows might have many long tunnels. They dig one large room for sleeping.

Badger sets usually have a lot of dirt and stones at the entrance. There is often a path leading to the set. Look for posts showing signs of scratching nearby. Badgers enjoy a good scratch with its front claws on a tree or stump.

FUN FACT!

In the winter, northern badgers **hibernate**. This means they sleep under the ground all winter long. Other badgers just rest a lot during the winter.

A Eurasian badger comes out of its home. A set often has a path leading to it and dirt and stones nearby.

Badgers like a clean, neat home. They carry in fresh clean grass to line their sleeping room. Badgers replace it when it seems stale or dirty. They even dig a special toilet outside the set. It is usually about 60 feet (18 m) away.

Because they are nocturnal, badgers are not seen often. They rarely leave their comfortable dens during the day. You might say a badger is shy. A badger will stay in its hole all night long if it thinks it is not safe to go out. It will also stay in if the night is dark and without much moonlight.

Badgers line their sleeping room with clean grass or flowers.

Baby Badgers

Baby badgers, or cubs, are born blind. Between one and five cubs are born at one time. They are only about 5 inches (13 cm) long at birth.

Cubs stay underground for six to eight weeks. When they finally come out, they don't go far. They scurry back to the set at the first sign of danger. But after a week, they feel braver. They begin to check out the area farther away. Soon the mother begins to take them out. They learn to hunt. After about eight months, cubs are ready to go off on their own.

FUN FACT!

Badgers have few enemies. Golden eagles, coyotes, cougars, and bobcats might attack a small badger. But the skin around a badger's neck is thick and muscular. This makes it hard for an enemy to grab.

Badgers dig fast! Badgers use their claws and strong front legs to reach a rodent underground. They have five long claws on their front feet. Their claws are about 2 inches (5 cm) long.

In soft soil, a badger works like a steam shovel! It uses its paws, claws, and teeth to move soil aside. A badger can dig deep enough to hide in minutes.

Badgers have great hearing and sense of smell. They hear and sniff out lunch even when it is underground. Then they quickly dig down to their meal. They have strong jaws.

FUN FACT!

Above ground, badgers pounce on **prey**. Sometimes badgers bury their meal. They will come back to snack on it later.

Badgers are some of the best diggers in the animal kingdom!

Stay Safe Around Badgers

Sometimes badgers like to live near where humans also live. Here are some steps you can take to make sure you and the badgers stay safe:

 Keep small house pets, like cats, indoors. This is especially important at night. Badgers will even attack lambs or other small animals.

 Install very bright motion-sensitive lights to discourage badgers from hanging out in your yard.

 Never let your dog chase a badger.

 Stay as far away from a badger as possible if you can.

 If you have animals like chickens on your property, bury your fence at least 12 or 18 inches (30 or 46 cm) deep. Remember, badgers are champion diggers!

Learn More

Books

Carr, Aaron. *Badgers*. New York: Weigl, 2015.

Maximus, Sofia. *Badgers in the Dark*. New York: Gareth Stevens, 2013.

Quinlan, Julia J. *Honey Badgers*. New York: PowerKids Press, 2013.

Roesser, Marie. *Honey Badgers*. New York: Gareth Stevens, 2014.

Sebastian, Emily. *Badgers*. New York: PowerKids Press, 2013.

Websites

Easy Science for Kids
easyscienceforkids.com/all-about-badgers/

Facts, photos, and links teach you even more about badgers.

Ohio Department of Natural Resources
wildlife.ohiodnr.gov/species-and-habitats/species-guide-index/mammals/american-badger

Head to this website for facts and photos about the American badger.

Index

Published in 2016 by Enslow Publishing, LLC.
101 W. 23rd Street, Suite 240, New York, NY 10011

Copyright © 2016 by Enslow Publishing, LLC.

Library of Congress Cataloging-in-Publication Data

Niver, Heather M. Moore, author.
 Badgers after dark / Heather M. Moore Niver.
   pages cm. — (Animals of the night)
 Audience: Ages 8+
 Audience: Grades 4 to 6.
 Includes bibliographical references and index.
 ISBN 978-0-7660-7168-1 (library binding)
 ISBN 978-0-7660-7166-7 (pbk)
 ISBN 978-0-7660-7167-4 (6-pack)
 1. Badgers—Juvenile literature. I. Title.
 QL737.C25N58 2016
 599.76'7—dc23

                    2015029915

Printed in the United States of America

To Our Readers: We have done our best to make sure all website addresses in this book were active and appropriate when we went to press. However, the author and the publisher have no control over and assume no liability for the material available on those websites or on any websites they may link to. Any comments or suggestions can be sent by e-mail to customerservice@enslow.com.

Photos Credits: Throughout book, narvikk/E+/Getty Images (starry background), kimberrywood/Digital Vision Vectors/Getty Images (green moon dingbat); cover, p. 1 Don Mammoser/Shutterstock.com (American badger), samxmed/E+/Getty Images (moon); p. 3 Mark Caunt/Shutterstock.com; p. 5 Eduard Kyslynskyy/Shutterstock.com; p. 7 Joe McDonald/Visuals Unlimited, Inc/Getty Images; p. 9 Jed Weingarten/National Geographic My Shot/Getty Images; p. 11 © Thailand Wildlife/Alamy; p. 13 Nzrst1jx/Wikimedia Commons/Meles meles anakuma at Inokashira Park Zoo.jpg/CC-BY-SA-3.0; p. 15 © Ch'ien C. Lee/wildborneo.com.my; p. 17 Johan-Swanepoel/Shutterstock.com; p. 19 Tom Murphy/National Geographic/Getty Images; p. 21 Dirk Freder/E+/Getty Images; p. 23 Laurie Campbell/The Image Bank/Getty Images; p. 25 Visuals Unlimited, Inc./Robert Pickett/Getty Images; p. 27 Cynthia Kidwell/Shutterstock.com; p. 29 John E Marriott/All Canada Photos/Getty Images.